THE BROKEN PLACES

The Broken Places

Sandy Coomer

Saddle Road Press

The Broken Places
© 2021 Sandy Coomer

Saddle Road Press
Ithaca, New York
saddleroadpress.com

All rights reserved. No part of this book may be reproduced or transmitted in any form or by any means without written permission of the author.

Designed by Don Mitchell
Cover image by Don Mitchell
Author photograph by Ashley Sarmiento

ISBN 978-1-7365258-0-7
Library of Congress Control Number 2021933313

Also by Sandy Coomer
Available Light

For my family—

*You've walked with me into the broken places
without a thought for the safety of your own heart.
You've helped me find my way out again.
"That's what family does."*

For Tim—

forever

The world breaks everyone,
and afterward, some are strong at the broken places.
—Ernest Hemingway

Contents

I Broken: World

To the Seashell	15
The Clock Master	17
Playing Dead	18
It's My Birthday and I'm Thinking About Death	19
Snake	20
After Goodnight	22
Pact	23
Into Morning	24
Deputy Finch	26
Running	28
Begonia	29
Seven Ways of Looking at a Shooting	30
Miss Landmine	31
How to Spell America	33
If Freedom	35

II Broken: Relationship

What Words Cost	39
Shadow Talk	40
Chance Encounter at Chevy's Back Alley Barbecue	42
Peacock Hill	43
If You Know What's Good for You	44
Facts About Lightning	45
I Compare Myself to Lot's Wife	46
A Dream	47
Study of Unknown Man at Laundromat	48
Shopping for Sweaters	49

INSTINCT	50
HEMATOLOGY	51

III Broken: Identity

MARBLES	55
EVE	56
PHOTOGRAPH	57
DISCOVERING SEX	58
POEM IN WHICH MY BODY IS A RANSOM	59
AFTER THREE CONGRESSMEN, TWO HIGH-PROFILE TV ANCHORS, AND A RADIO HOST LOSE THEIR JOBS DUE TO ACCUSATIONS OF SEXUAL MISCONDUCT, I HAVE A DREAM	60
HOPE	62
EVE DECIDES MOTHERHOOD IS NOT ALL IT'S CRACKED UP TO BE	63
PAPER DOLL	64
THE BODY IS WISE LIKE THIS	65
EVE CONTEMPLATES A NAME CHANGE	66
STUDY OF WOMAN IN CHILD'S POSE	67
DEFINITION OF MIDDLE AGE	68
THE DANCER CONFRONTS THE PORTRAIT PAINTER	70
UNPACKING THE BODY MIRACLE	71
TO THE HUMAN BARBIE, FROM BARBIE	73
THERAPY	74
FAR AWAY PLACES	76

IV Broken: Body

MONSIEUR DEGAS IS GOING BLIND	81
FROM THE BALCONY	82
FLIGHT	84
LAUNDRY	86
MIRAGE	87
IN SICKNESS	88
SOMETHING IN WALKING	90

WHITE MAGIC	92
VOCABULARY	93
INSOMNIA POEM	94
HUNGER	95
AIRPORT PAT-DOWN	96
TELLING THE FAMILY THERE IS NOTHING MORE THEY CAN DO	97

V BROKEN: HEART

ARS POETICA	101
MORNING PRACTICE	102
LETTER TO DAVID FROM ONYX CAVE	104
GHOSTS USE LOGIC TO CONVINCE MY MOTHER THEY EXIST	105
TANGLES	106
DARKER	108
NIGHTFALL	109
WAITING	110
IN MY DREAM	111
TRAVELING NORTH WITH GRIEF	112
POISON IVY	113
WHAT I CARRY	115
ADVICE AFTER LOSING A SPOUSE	116
RE-WILDING	118
TO MAKE SENSE OF THIS WORLD AGAIN	119
NOTES	121
ACKNOWLEDGEMENTS	124
SPECIAL THANKS	126
ABOUT THE AUTHOR	127

I Broken: World

Is it anyone's fault this world has teeth?

To the Seashell

that traveled
ocean depths
and landed
on this narrow shore,
this poem is yours.
You've come unbidden,
unmoored, a flip
upon a wave of time.
Who would've guessed
today I'd walk
barefoot in cold surf,
jeans rolled up
to my knees,
looking for a miracle?
Is it anyone's business
I prefer to speak
my tragedies
to the water's roar?
Is it anyone's fault
this world has teeth?
Even the surf
with its foamy edge
eats away at the beach.
But you, tiny calcium
mantle, the elemental
flash of your white spiral
redeems me.
Your open ear
welcomes the hushed
tremors of my breath.
Why does it matter
so much you appeared?

And why did I stop,
carry you home,
like you were
everything
I ever needed?

The Clock Master

The master cleans the Breslin Tower clock.
The village groans under the stall of time
between the looming clouds and circling hawk.

A clock without its face, it causes talk
of sure disaster, an unlucky sign.
The master cleans the Breslin Tower clock

as townsfolk wander, stop to stare and gawk
at driving chains, the bell striker, the line
between the looming clouds and circling hawk.

Minutes freeze and hours choke and lock
and children cling to mothers' skirts and hide
as the master cleans the Breslin Tower clock.

The bravest men are turning into rock,
their faces wide and white like painted mimes
beneath the looming clouds and circling hawk.

Frozen in a space of scourge and shock,
the village slows and fades as sleep arrives.
The master cleans the Breslin Tower clock
and grins at looming clouds and circling hawk.

Playing Dead

We took turns playing dead, laid out on the coffee table
the way the old encyclopedia showed black-suited men

after disease or duels. We knew nothing except to be still
and cross one hand atop the other like we were shielding

our stopped hearts. I posed you, straightened your legs,
aligned your ankles, knees, hips, smoothed your T-shirt

of wrinkles, tucking the too-big sides underneath your shoulders
so that your thin chest was squared and flat as an unread bible.

I ran fingers over your face and placed pennies on your eyelids.
I slicked your corn-silk hair with spit, tucked wayward strands

behind your ears and pronounced you dead.
You took one deep chest of air and held it.

Even as your heart beat a steady *I'm-alive* rhythm,
the quiet of your body took the weight of dark rock or wet wood

and pressed a strange resistance out of my throat. I squeezed
it back and counted the dead moments until I was sure

you'd been dead longer than me. I called you the winner.
Through the window, the bright sun urged another game

and we scrambled outside, where no shadow could claim my face,
nor one of those brief surges of love that drown the heart

for no particular reason.

It's My Birthday and I'm Thinking About Death

because who knows what the year will hold
wrapped up in its sparkly paper and curly bows.
Sometimes a bright package holds something
you never wanted. Long underwear. House slippers.
A purple paisley scarf. Even if I promise to take
every day as it comes, offer myself to morning
like a sacrifice, genetics may very well undo me.
There are men that expect to die in their fifties
with the heart disease of their fathers, grandfathers.

Death can come suddenly, like the swoop of a hawk
or the bold strike of a rattlesnake, and there's no
way to avoid it. Remember that waiter in Chicago
who slipped in spilled water and hit his head
on the table edge? And how about the cyclist
sideswiped by a pickup, the driver chatting gaily
on a cell phone. Even the ant crawls unsuspectingly
out of the hill with every intention to carry 100 times
its body weight, only to be crushed under a boot.

There's a party planned at my favorite restaurant.
There will be wine and cake, and I will laugh
with my friends who tell me I look ten years younger
than I am. But just in case there's spilled water
on the floor tonight and I go the way of the waiter,
just in case there's a driver texting his girlfriend
right when I'm crossing the street, I'll ask my family
to delete my Facebook account. No need for my birthday
to come up next year in anyone's reminders—
like yours did—
and with it, a white flash of pain, your life a sparkler
that flared brightest right before it burned out.

Snake

Rat snake, my husband said.
King snake, my neighbor said.

    Either way, a good snake.
    Keep it around, let it snake

around the yard, kill mice, kill
copperheads. But we killed

    it—a shovel to the brain.
    I didn't watch the quivering body, brain

still firing the final twitches.
I had seen it strike! The twitching

    tongue. Something in the way
    it curved its body upon itself weighs

on me. The grip of danger, the fear
it must have felt—my fear.

    What primordial grasp came upon
    my heart to make it race on

like that? An enemy? A coil
of inhabited evil, uncoiled

    along its scales? I saw
    shed skin under the table, saw

the black length of it in the corner
and then it saw me cornered

    and it fled. How shocked we both appeared.
    I couldn't let it disappear

knowing what it knew—this house
and all the ways fear is housed

> inside us. It knew the way back in
> and so the shovel halved its back.

So far is a deep thing remembered
and I could not abide that memory.

After Goodnight

I am playing a guitar
and watching you
move your hips
to the rhythm
of river and flood.

You swirl in a pool,
bend to pick up
a dark stone
and send it skipping
across the smooth sound
of ache and bone.

What did we think
about pain
and what did we know
about contracts
and promises?

Changing our minds
is for the innocent
and it's much too late
for that now.

Pact

We're standing on a bridge
over a swollen river,
watching the dead dance in the undercurrent,
their white shirts fluttering like wings.

Send word to the strong dark timber buckling
under our feet, water-logged and earthy.

Send word to the rust on our fingertips,
the frizzle in our hair.

We have an urge to leave.

Our dark eyes reflect the moon
and the smooth ladder of our ribs
is set for climbing.

Don't listen to nightingales.

Let the crust of their sand-raked promises
fall into the water.

The dead are hungry for words that taste like
lemon and basil, that have the consistency
of foam.

When we fall to the river's face
and empty our hands of all that we carry,
let's speak water-deep in tongues.

Send word to the mourning doves
to learn a new song.

Send word to our mothers—
we aren't coming back.

Into Morning

We wring our hands
and set our throats
to sea.

You carry
a soft patchwork quilt
stitched

with last words.
There is no regret,
you say,

but you have to say that, don't you?

Otherwise, the fog
that lines the trees
would rot and turn

to mushrooms.
Underneath, there is
only a burrow of worms.

The earth is too soft for me.
Give me acid rain.
Give me a place

to rake my fingers in sand
and follow a path out of here.
Get me a plastic bag and a knife.

Get me a belt and a gallon
of gasoline. Get me a hose
and masking tape.

The stars keep watching
for a way out
of the night.

If they can hold their breath
a little while longer,
morning will open its eyes.

Deputy Finch

how did you know
what to say
when you found the boy
standing on the outside
of the railing, 145 feet
over cold concrete

the bridge suddenly
narrow, the night
strange and stark
how did you know
to walk measured
not rattled or rushed

was it your police
training or was it
how much you loved
your own son
sleeping in that moment
unaware of life's
awful failings

and how this boy
with his fists
gripped around the bars
was everything
you feared and dreaded
for every mixed-up
sad boy trying to find
a way out of his pain

how did you know
confessing
you were scared too
would prove something

so vital, the boy
would reach out his hand
barely visible
in the scattered dark
but enough to hold onto
and not let go

Running

after the 2018 school shooting in Parkland, Florida

They will tear down the school this summer,
so that no child will ever have to run through
that hallway again. All those children running.

That slick floor. The light at the end of the hall.
The afternoon breaking into pieces of glass.
The pop pop pop of the breaking. The running.

I tell the doctor I limp when I run and there is a pop
of pain in my hip. The X-ray says arthritis.
The doctor says, see this space, how little is left.
It's going to hurt. All that running.

They will tear every classroom down. The gym
and cafeteria. The office. The theatre. The band room.
They will run every nightmare into the street,
every memory into the ground. All that running.

Let's try this. The doctor guides a needle into my hip.
This will dull the pain. He shoots my hip full of cortisone.
The pop pop pop of the shooting. No more running, he says.

All those children running. All those rooms.
They will tear them down. They will dull the pain.
Brick by brick by terrible brick, that building will fall.
The pop pop pop of the falling.

There's a lot of damage, the doctor says.
You'll never be the same.

Begonia

after the 2017 church shooting in Smyrna, Tennessee

After the incident at church, you pay more attention
to the garden, especially the plant growing wild
in the dirt beside the manse.

Wide, well-veined leaves of soft green
disguise the blood-red reverse.

Weeks ago, you thought *begonia*
but waited until the delicate pink blooms
lifted out of the fold to name it.

You drop to your knees to study the botany of begonia
and wonder about the need to name everything,

to label it, when so much is unknowable—
ordinary, steady on one side,
bloody on the other.

You still have nightmares about the shooter,
who everyone said was a swell guy

until they saw the reverse of him—
the dead woman in the parking lot,
the pastor with bullets in his arms.

How can you name the flight that took your legs
even as your heart pleaded *go back, find your friends*?

You confess courage is two-sided,
fragmented, a label only found in the dirt.
You kneel in the drifting shade

and try to understand yourself,
which means to understand humanity,

which cannot be understood,
no matter what name you give its wildest part,
the hard, blunt face of its blooming.

Seven Ways of Looking at a Shooting

1. Circle, circle, pool of molten lava
   congealed at the rim, the scent of metal,
   smoke, a piece of wood smoldering.

2. Stick figure drawn on paper, an outline
   of a sentence, the modifiers dangling like legs.

3. A phone call, a family, blue lights, white lights,
   a flashing yellow, an echo, a morning of ash.

4. What do we do with this city when a man
   can't walk in his own neighborhood,
   when a man can't walk, when a man can't.

5. Statistics and numbers and counting.
   Someone in city hall knows the percentages,
   equations, multiplication, square roots
   and subtraction, subtraction.

6. Morgue-cold, metal trays, a face beneath
   a sheet, a toe tag, a funeral home, a grave.

7. Question: Can you blame him? Yes.
   Question: Can you blame him? No.
   We turn circles. We speak lava.
   We start over from the beginning.

Miss Landmine

It doesn't matter that you were only twelve
when you stepped down at the edge of the river
to the sound of your leg blasting apart.
That sound still wakes you from deepest sleep
sometimes, when the ache in your stump
won't resolve. Memories mar the present
if you let it, but you fight not to let it,
hopping with your crutch to the market,
your white skirt brushing against your one knee.

And neither does the twenty-five years
of civil war matter anymore, the Russian rifles
and the American politicians, now that
ten years of peace is celebrated with parties
and parades, even a beauty pageant
with lovely amputees lined along the stage.
Fuchsia, magenta, emerald gowns radiate
the room, as contestants tuck orchids behind
ears and straighten bejeweled tiaras.

A sash of silver satin sweeps the chest,
spelling the proud hometown. One will claim
a crown, a new prosthetic leg and the title
Miss Landmine. Part of you thinks this is
brilliant and brave. Another part cringes
as you listen to the women explain
the circumstance of their maiming: tending
fields, escaping from an attacking soldier,
gathering water at the river.

Just gathering water in a jar at the river—
that sound, the blood, the white jag of bone,
your horrified friends running for help, leaving
you with your life spilling against the sand.

Those memories fade now as the winner poses and the cameras flash. The reporters ask how it feels to not be a victim anymore, and the winner speaks the words *survive*, *endure*, straight into your heart.

How to Spell America

I point to words in the reading book and she bends
her mouth to letters, her soft voice persistent
behind teeth and tongue. Her eyes are dark, intense
like an owl's, and she weaves the forest of language
with the pencil she holds in her hand.
>*What do you buy at the post office?*
>*Which one of these pictures is a stamp?*

I speak slowly and give each letter an exaggerated sound.
P makes a different sound than *B*. With *P*, you must push
the air away like you push away bad dreams and memories.
With *B*, you cradle the sound in your arms like a child.
> Her son is 12 years, 3 months old. Her daughter
> is 8 years, 7 months old. They have lived
> in the apartment for 2 years, 6 months. She is on
> page 58 of the reading book. She speaks Arabic at home.
> Her husband is too tired at night to check her homework.

Arabic has 8 vowel sounds. English has 22 vowel sounds.
Arabic speakers studying English often switch *B* for *P* and *F* for *V*.
The *TH* sound is especially difficult.

I tell her another word for ID is identification. 6 syllables. 6 sounds.
A long, complicated word. We say the syllables one at a time.
I show her my driver's license. I tell her this is my identification.
It's an important word. If you know this word,
you know who you are.
> *At the bank, we make a deposit. Put money in.*
> *At the bank, we make a withdrawal. Take money out.*
> She deposits her life in America.
> She withdraws a home, a job, a family.

I turn to the picture of the neighborhood and she points
to each building when I say its name. She is proud to show me
what she knows. Her eyes are glitter and light. When she
can read English she can apply for a job in the school cafeteria.
Show me the flower shop. Show me the bakery.
I am in the grocery store. I am in the library.

We look up the word *community* in the English to Arabic
translator app on my phone. She laughs, repeats the word.
It floats on her lips, then rushes into the air like an eager bird.

In Arabic, adjectives follow nouns. There are no silent letters.
In Arabic, there is no present tense for the verb *to be*.

If Freedom

If freedom were a bird
>would it swoop from the swirling thermals
>and hover above a field of buttercups? Would it perch
>on a rocky outcrop, nod its wise head to questions
>the wind posed? Would it sit with me as I sing
>by a campfire, sparks rising into the vast night?

Maybe it's too easy to gift freedom with glossy, glittery wings.

Better to give it weight, the way a man on a tractor loves his land
like his children, knows the burden of horizon, the edge of fence
bending a small hill to a flat creek.

Better to give it frenzy, like a woman dancing in a meadow,
skirts iridescent and shimmering, spinning the orbit of the moon.

If freedom were a field of knee-high grass gone to seed,
>let every gate stay open.

If freedom were furrows on a hot summer day,
>let the earth be rich enough to grow whatever's planted,
>harvest whatever grows.

If freedom were a flag,
>let it fly colorless, high enough to join circling hawks.

Let it take the hue of rain, which is falling now, clean and cool,
on the man riding his tractor, his hands turning the big machine
home, the mowed rows straight as honest conversation.

It's falling on the woman and her upturned face. She's laughing,
tasting persimmon and rose on the sky-washed breeze.

If freedom were philosophy
>would it light on my shoulder and whisper advice?
>Would it say don't buy any more rope for your dreams,
>no more screws? Would it say locks are for cages,
>walls for enclosed rooms?

This heart is lonely for clover and violets, the buzz
of honeybee in the cherry trees. All I know is this thirst
for space—the kind I gulp until I'm full, like a night
beaded with stars.

If freedom is an illusion, a mirage, a myth,
> then this poem is a mirror, a surrender
> into the only things worth keeping—a high meadow,
> an open sky, body and mind circling the other's secrets,
> obliged to stare and wonder
>
> how anything can be this wild, this beautiful.

II Broken: Relationship

*We look at our hands and know what they're capable of.
We know what they've already done.*

What Words Cost

Back then, we understood what words were worth.
My sister and I, in our shared bed,

wrote silent messages to each other as evening
deepened to night.

My fingers spelled magic into the soft creases of her palm,
and she, eyes closed, let it form

beneath her eyelids—letters connected by touch, the circle
of O, the almost square of E.

I watched her concentrate until the word emerged
from skin one letter at a time,

was mouthed into existence—*horse, dollhouse, grass, pillow*—
soft words that blanketed

the sharp, angled syllables of our parents arguing downstairs.
My sister held my hand open

and conjured *cake, river,* let the letters take the weight
of not knowing by becoming known

behind the curtain of our childhood—*plate, feather, window.*
It seemed simple,

not speaking, trusting the hands that made speaking
unnecessary. Or maybe

we were careful—what words we shared, what we asked
each other to hold.

We knew the value of silence. Once spoken, words
could cost everything.

Shadow Talk

I watched
your shadow shift
on the bedroom wall,
your hands gesturing,
your torso
hunched with anger.
I tried to hear your words,
really I did,
but the truth of your anger
played out best
in the dark theatre
of your body.
A response from me
seemed unnecessary,
and you, who would never
admit there was any other way
to feel, didn't wait for one.
It seemed prudent,
polite even,
to watch your raised arms
and wild hair cover
my sunken silhouette,
to fade further into silence.

Forgive me
for baring my shadow hands
when you turned your head,
for digging at your neck
with curved claws.
Forgive me for standing,
dwarfing you on the wall,
blotting you out
with my giant face.

I had to loom
as large as possible
to remind myself I mattered.
It had nothing to do with you.

Chance Encounter at Chevy's Back Alley Barbecue

They stood beside each other in the parking lot of the restaurant—the one he loves, the one she always hated, and now hates even more after spying him with his new family in the torn corner booth. He had followed her retreat outside to ask how she'd been the last three years, or maybe to show her he'd made something of himself. It wasn't how he thought it would be. The words didn't form. Instead, they floated unsaid and fell in the gravel at his feet. For some crazy reason, he wanted to touch her, but the small reach toward her hand provoked a flinch, a deep inhale as if she needed to prepare herself to be wounded again. And then it was dark, and he thought it fitting the day decided to shut its sunny mouth and pour the rest of the hours in the drainage ditch. Dead is dead, she said when she spoke of their past and he agreed, then turned his back like a wall against her, though he couldn't bring himself to leave. They stood silent, remembering the bodies they used to be. Love, or the loss of it, still carried its shape in the shimmery air. Hickory smoke floated into the cloudless night.

Peacock Hill

What if we give up on forgiveness and instead
    walk through the brambles to the top of the rise
        and watch the wild peacocks roost in the trees.
Turquoise and emerald, fringed and crested cobalt—
    let's soak our eyes in color and kneel in the dirt, tune
        ourselves with the infrasonic music of their wings.
We've been too long splintered and bandaged.
    Who bought that ax we shoulder between us,
        those scales that weigh our sins like the city measures
garbage hauled from office parks?
    If you need to find my weakness, I'll lay it before you
        and write its story in blood. You won't be surprised
by the dozen eyes, the luster of plum and gold.
    I am, after all, a figment of what you think I am.
        Let's climb the trees and lie in the canopy of night
and whisper our secrets to the peahens.
    They know enough of love to give us good advice.
        Look how patiently they sit on their nest of eggs
while coyotes sneer beyond the field of feathers.
    Hold an egg in your hand and paint our resurrection.
        No matter what you think about our chances,
let morning find us iridescent and shimmering.

If You Know What's Good for You

But I don't, so I move a little closer
to the wall to listen to my neighbors.
I sense, or maybe I just imagine,
love in the room beyond the too-thin
barrier between us. This is the apartment
where I swore I'd keep to myself,
stay hidden, not learn anyone's name
or share my own, not open the door
to anyone needing a teaspoon of vanilla
extract, triple-A batteries, a lightbulb.
But I don't know what's good for me,
and her name, my neighbor, is Sue,
and right now, Sue is loving her boyfriend
and from the sound of it, being loved back.
I wrap my arms around myself and think
about Sue, just yesterday, with the blue-bruise
imprint of a hand around her thin arm asking
if I could lend her ten bucks. I dug in my purse,
found fifteen, pressed it into her palm
just a little too long for her not to know
how thin these walls are, how curses thud
darkly and breaking glass slices the night,
how *if you know what's good for you*
can echo in your head for months, maybe
even years—because we don't, Sue.
We never do.

Facts About Lightning

To the five hundred people struck
last year, a poem is the last thing
you want to read, but please indulge me.
Let's talk about fingers and nerve endings
and how we know language by the way
words feel in our mouths. This poem is about
intense attraction. Don't make me say
    flash or *streak* or *buzz.*
I will say
    razor and *feather* and *ricochet*—
demonstrate how passion rewires neurons
the same way flames leap across fields.

We saw the clouds tumbling in the west
before the omen that was our voices traveled
at one-third the speed of light—
all two hundred million volts of it.
We saw the damage, the flashover
we'd do to our polarized bodies.
There is a dark cave inside our ribs
that has no name except
    vacant and *energy* and *afterburn.*

We are dangerous together. We know that.
We know that silence after a flare creates
a certain pattern of scars, like tree limbs
or a sentence diagram. There's no need
to discuss the plasma trail, the bursting
blood vessels. We look at our hands
and know what they're capable of.
We know what they've already done.

I Compare Myself to Lot's Wife

Can you blame me
for looking back on our life?
I didn't believe God would frown
on reminiscing. When you say
now I've ruined everything,
let me point out it wasn't my idea
to wander. I was content in our house
of sadness, the wind chimes worrying
the cedars.

Latch on to a thick grapevine,
wrap it around your forearm
and follow it to water.
Build a house under sycamores
beside a rambling creek.
Think of me dancing in the fire
of distant stars. I will flavor
your soup with the spice
of my eyes and serve it
to your lovers as a warning.

A Dream

I awoke to an answered question. –Thoreau

My lover is a fish—

his belly iridescent in the sun
his mouth a dark cave,
his eyes, two coins that never stop staring.

The stream is full of tumbled rocks

split from upstream boulders.
Rushes line the low bank and a garter snake
coils in the shade. I stand knee deep,

the tugging current like a sentence that needs saying.

My lover's gills churn a watery breath
and from his throat, nothing but the sound
of shattering glass.

We layer our lives

with the songs of crickets and tree frogs.
We open our mouths to a basalt sky,
tracing a road map of scars with our tongues.

The water is cold and my feet are numb.

My lover shifts, all shimmer and fin.
He watches me from his pebble bed,
stirring the sand with his glossy tail.

I scoop him with a net, toss him

to the grass and let the dry air sting
his throat until he heaves truth. Words fall
from his broken mouth like sparks from a fire,

and finally, an awakening.

Study of Unknown Man at Laundromat

You decide he's happy living alone. You watch
as he folds clothes and stacks them neatly
on the counter. Maybe he's given up on marriage,
companionship, though not on the idea of love.
It's likely he offered his heart once, twice,
was sent home packing. It's hard to come back
from that. You look over the fading sky as it blues
the fields, the tree line thick like the grip
you feel sometimes behind your breastbone.
You wonder if he feels it too, dismisses it,
like you do, as heartburn from last night's takeout.

You can tell a person's mood by their breathing—
a long exhale, a letting go of all the private dark.
Love has a way of digging in fingernail deep.
It's hard to wrench away without blood.
He's happy, he seems happy, and who are you
to doubt it, you who never folded your laundry
so perfectly square and cornered, who'd
just as soon skip the folding step altogether,
dig clothes from the basket, wrinkled and messy.
The man leaves. You lift another load to the dryer,
the humid heat and whirring spin cycle
dizzying your mind, the futile act of cleaning
a little more painful than it should be.

Shopping for Sweaters

I watch her hold it to her chest,
measuring the fit, shell pink
against narrow shoulders,
ribbed cuff at wrist.

I ask about the frayed neckline
and hem. She says, *distressed*,
which is the style now, ruined
on purpose to make a statement.

I examine the little bites
taken out of the weave, what
a moth would do in a closet,
dark eyes, the brush of wings.

I ask if the edges will further
unravel and she shrugs as if to say
it doesn't matter, as if to remind me
she's alone again, starting over,

her life like a pile of discards
on the changing room floor.
She wears the past like a rip,
torn by hands that forgot

how to fold and stack. We move
to the scarves, crimson and rust,
what she'll wear at her throat
against the coming cold.

Instinct

Rescued, I take the feral cat to the work shed.
I'm supposed to contain him for two weeks, feed him,
talk to him, convince him he's safe. He's calm.
He eats, lets me scratch his bony shoulders.

My child is the farthest away from me she's ever been.
She says the days in Anchorage are short, the air
so cold her lungs rattle with frost. She works twelve-hour
shifts. Between the bay and the glaciers, she's healing.

Gone is muggy Tennessee with its slow heavy days,
it's shallow creeks meandering like an old woman
perusing the sales rack. My child laughs when we talk
on the phone, but I can't tell if she means it

without seeing her eyes. The cat's eyes are honey
and citrus. He curls around my legs purring until I
open the shed door and he tastes the bright promise
of a different kind of safety. He lopes along the fence line,

across the unmowed field. The lady at the shelter sent
instructions—*What to do if your feral cat escapes*—
almost as if she knew he would. A bitter water distills
in me. I pick dandelions, the flowers gone to seed.

I watch the cat leap tall weeds, his sleek back smooth
in pale sun. I leave food, prop the door open, call a name
he never wore as his own. I want to believe he knows
where home is, but I don't think he's ever coming back.

Hematology

I remember galaxies
and the blank night of stars
we stood under
when we sliced our palms with a razor blade
you stole from your father's sink.

We mingled our blood
and swore sweet words we believed
would last. We tangled
our bodies as the aurora undulated in the dark
and we believed in love,

that every breath
we took was as much the other's as our own.
We were that young,
walking across the brittle glass
of our lives.

The blood on the grass
marked our path like the invisible lines
between Orion, the Lion, the Bear.
There are five million blood cells in a drop of blood—
this is fact—

neutrophils and lymphocytes,
red cells, the tiny bubbled platelets gathered
like grapes among grapefruit.
We were that innocent. We were that desperate.
The blade of our promises

carved the sound of moonlight
from water, the musky scent of wet night from skin.
The palms we split red
faded into scar, into memory, like a pulse
of starlight—first brilliant

then barely there at all.

III Broken: Identity

I ask my uterus what is the nature of being female
and she answers with the messy particulars of blood

Marbles

My daughter designs herself with marbles—
blue pearlies for eyes, an oxblood for nose,
her mouth a line of comets and galaxies
for the orbit of words she speaks.

The shape of her body on the carpet,
colorful, unique, a Picasso by mibster—
I hope she remembers this when the world
takes a turn at the art of her image.

Her head shimmers, like a star, to claim
a future she doesn't yet name—onionskin
and corkscrew, mica and swirly—the thin places
that can haunt her, the turns she can't predict.

Her tiger arms are strong enough to hold her
on this ledge of self, sturdy enough
to knuckle down with her silver steely fingers
studded with pale clearie fingertips.

Her legs are long—dragonfly and cricket,
butterfly, bumblebee. She's solid
and steady, run worthy, nimble enough
for masher and crock, red devil, cat's eye.

My daughter lies on the carpet, poses
beside her other body. I measure her against
my fears—what girls will face circling the outside
of a ring. She laughs and rakes her hand

through the alleys and aggies, ducks and taws.
The sunburst of her face scatters to the wall
and she lets them roll. I gather them into a pile,
guard them, fiercely. I don't want to tell her yet

this world always plays for keeps.

Eve

A palette of green,
moss and sage, she stands
in the garden to test
the earth, judge
the drumbeat of plum
and blackberry, the heat
of peppers on the low shrub.
Every leaf is a balance
between harsh and yielding,
the stem shifting supple
to stiff. She is a blend
of blood and spine, curve
and arrow, a flower pressed
in a thick book. Her face
sustains a willowy edge,
innocence and knowledge,
a blend of conflicting
songs, the oval seeds
in her drawn-tight center

a cluster of living stones.

Photograph

In this photograph
I am fifteen and a woman
with curves I have not quite
fit into yet—hips still narrow
and waist still rib-thin,
thighs lacking the roundness
a man could grip, and at my feet,
the leaves of shucked corn,
all green and crisp, and in my hands
the yellow cob like a prize I've won
at the county fair. I don't remember
the reason my mother took
this picture, though I suppose
it was to remember me in the bud,
tight like a flower plucked before bloom,
ready to spread in a mason jar of water.
This was two years before I wed,
before the first baby and the fullness
my body would know. The shape
of my future is spelled in fat letters
someone wrote in the sky above me.
Harvest, it says, in an ink that faded
over the years, like the corn silk I braided
and used as a bookmark to hold
my place in this ripped-down world.

Discovering Sex

In the garden between rows
of newly green lettuces
curled leaves overlapping
so tight at the center unloosing
the frilled fragrance of soil
as the green deepens ripens opens readies

we are both unsure if we can breathe

the sweet peas climbing the shaky trellis
the tendrils slipping between the slats
to latch a breath, a gasp

the whole earth shudders beneath us

the blood-red tomatoes fruit heavy and full
the flowering summer squash yellow sweet
cones of nectar cords of vine
radishes carrots peppers corn
moan under moonlight
dancing crimson gold the molten deep
the hidden seed the melon in the dirt
the coarse weight and mounded flesh

and ours

we rise

the earth knows our secrets
the silent depths that gather us
back again and back again.

Poem in Which My Body is a Ransom

The note says *thighs* and *shoulders*, *mouth* and *eyes*.
I wait tables at an upscale restaurant in Belle Meade. I'm eighteen

with an invitation to spend a day with a forty-year-old man—
play tennis, dine at the country club. Here's his card.

Anthony builds houses, drinks bourbon at the bar,
drives a Porsche, smiles with dark eyes, trick eyes. He calls me

beautiful.

I bring his food on a round white plate. He tips well. I need money
for college. I am a flame-thrower. My heat strips the night.

I am a cracked window, a broken latch, an empty cupboard,
a lost key. I am a vision, Anthony says. He leaves me love notes,

beautiful eyes.

I am a dark cavern, a lonely owl in the night. I am a tattoo
of birds that fly up and off my arms.

I keep Anthony's card in a drawer by my bed.

Anthony is waiting at the front door of the restaurant.
Anthony is watching me count tip money.

I am a tidal wave wrecking the shore.
I am a fish—flesh and scales. I am bait.

I am a river cutting the canyon, train tracks running
between coasts. I am learning how it feels to be a woman,

and a man is a man is a man is a man is a
man.

After Three Congressmen, Two High-Profile TV Anchors, and a Radio Host Lose Their Jobs Due to Accusations of Sexual Misconduct, I Have a Dream

I run on a paved trail in a manicured park
near my subdivision. I don't think about

being groped or how I'd respond to cat-calls
with the quip *I could be your mother.*

I don't worry, even as I wipe the sweat
from my eyes, that someone is staring

because everyone is doing what I'm doing—
running—though there are some walkers too,

and a man trying to learn how to ride a bicycle.
His mother calls *you can do it* over and over.

I run toward him carefully and he pedals toward me
not so carefully. I watch where his eyes are pointed

because I know by experience when one person
is heading toward another person, it takes planning

not to crash. My body flexes to accept the expected,
but the man sees me, swerves at the last moment,

the lines of concentration widening to a startled *oh*
as he loses his balance and wiggle-woggles

off the pavement. He tips and slumps, lands
with the soft thud a body makes falling into grass.

His mother rushes past me and I want to say
it isn't my fault. (But that's obvious, right?)

I keep running, and though the mother in me wants
to look back to make sure they are both ok, I don't.

I look down like I am searching for something I lost
or maybe something the man lost though I have no idea

what that could be. It could be anything, it could be nothing,
but I can't shake the feeling it's something we both want back.

Hope

after the painting by Gustav Klimt, 1907-8

One arm to shield yourself
from the dark skull crouching at your belly,
your face bows, eyes closed,
your orange shawl engraved like a shield.

You ward off the spirits of blood and loss
that plucked your last baby from your body
like a crow snatching bright glass.

You press your forehead to the wall, praying.
You lie on your side, fetal-curled, praying.

Already you love too much the beauty
inside you. You pre-mourn the future
with three faces tucked into your gown.
A colorful weeping.

A thought flutters in your hands, folding
the cloth in a hushed Amen. A second chance.
You open your eyes to music, a faint song
you name hope.

Stars swarm the gold and blistering field,
brighter and all around you.

Eve Decides Motherhood Is Not All It's Cracked Up to Be

After the first two, the others came swiftly. Every year,
another hungry newborn rooting for her breast.

Adam delights in his offspring, spawning the first generation
of a new world, and God seems content to watch from his throne,

grinning at the playful antics of toddlers and preschoolers,
the first fumbles of hormone-driven adolescents.

For Eve, the days are long and the nights longer. She can't recall
the last time she slept for two uninterrupted hours,

or when she went to the bathroom without a voice shouting
Mommy. It's not that she doesn't love her children. She does.

But she's tired and her back aches. The lines around her eyes
are deep and the stretch marks on her belly, feathery white.

Some days, it's all she can do to stop herself from opening
the front door and setting off in whatever direction seems easiest—

one foot down, then the other, until she can't see the house
or hear the kids. She tries to talk to Adam about the symptoms

of depression. He sternly reminds her life is all about sacrifice
and he works hard to support them all.

Sacrifice, she thinks, as the baby inside kicks her ribs.
Every day she carries their sins and pardons again and again,

every birth, her body broken, her blood poured out for them.

Paper Doll

I cut myself out of paper.
The outline of my body
is a thick black line against
the white hollow of sky.

Every cut I make takes
a layer of living, quick
dreams drowned in a bath
of hurt. What I have left
is a surface of fieldstone
interspersed with fallen trees,
the brown glaze of a fencepost
and barbed wire.

I know where the blackberries
grow thorns inside a purple maze.
I skirt the rock face and follow
the small stream to the pond
where dragonflies skim algae.
Daffodils return in March,
covering the slope behind the barn.
Sawdust is as good as glitter
in my hair and the brush of sun
on my cheeks, a glow of rose.

I free the rounded curves
of my shoulders, the slight
rise of my chest, the map
of my belly, my slender legs.
The paper bark of birch
is the boat I load my heart into,
cut to strips so thin they blow
like cottonwood seed
on the back of the storm
that's coming.

The Body is Wise Like This

The body roils with pain like an ocean,
cold foam at its edge.

The body is fluent in Latin, a language of origin,
the base for all its babble.

The body floats on the back of a gray whale
that pauses, briefly, before it breaches.

The body circles with vultures on the backbone
of the wind, spirals hot and rises like bread.

The body hovers in its wind-swept house,
stands in the doorway as the windows cry.

The body crouches in the ditch it dug for itself,
takes comfort in the luxury of dirt, the scent of loam.

The body isn't skilled at pretending,
tells the mind to keep imagination to itself.

The body urges caution to its members,
confesses there are many kinds of emptiness.

Eve Contemplates a Name Change

Eve watches a sparrow build a nest in the window box.
It flies back and forth carrying wisps of dry grass in its beak,
weaving a neat bed, and stopping every now and then to tilt
its face skyward and chirp a cheery good morning. Eve smiles.
She respects a sunny disposition mixed with a healthy work ethic.
Purpose and passion, she thinks, earth and sky, grounded and free.

Something has been troubling her for some time now.
She's concerned about how she's portrayed in the media.
Medieval art hasn't treated her kindly. In almost every canvas,
she's posed in the garden. A snake either dangles from a tree limb
in front of her or crawls in the dirt at her feet. She is sick and tired
of being linked with serpents. Except for that one unfortunate day,
she has never spoken to reptiles.

Eve wants the world to know there is more to her
than what is depicted on parchment or canvas. She is free-spirited
and quick-witted, a problem solver and a juggler of many schedules.
She can knead bread and call out spelling words at the same time.
She can change a diaper with one hand. And she can sing—
lullabies and show tunes both.

She fingers the Legal Change of Name form she picked up
from the county clerk's office. Carefully, she fills it out
with steady clear handwriting. Under the heading, New Name,
she hesitates, taps the line with her quill, just as the sparrow
explodes with song. She watches it twitter at the edge of the nest,
confident and bold. With one flap of wing, it lifts to open blue.
Eve smiles again. Call me Bird, she says aloud.

Study of Woman in Child's Pose

she wants the ground to claim her
so she presses her forehead to its heart

the scent of damp earth and root
a joining of knots
        a deeper tangle

she wants to be found in shadow
broken   then reclaimed in light

the way a seed is rescued
by its ruptured skin
        the green reaching sunward

maybe it's not necessary to love the child she was
maybe that's too much to expect

her hips open   her chest at rest on her thighs
she wants to pour herself into the ground

learn a new language she never thought possible

a dark forgiveness
        but soft like skin

Definition of Middle Age

part lonely, part alone
part cascading waterfall
part boiling river
see: dangerous
see: color of minerals
    malachite green
    lapis lazuli blue
I write in a notebook
and on the cover
    is a picture of a llama

a red-headed woodpecker
fifty feet high in a coastal pine
clings as it drills for insects

I am fifty years into my life
see: mid century
see also: tide, going out
see also: moon, waning

the pine leans at an unlikely angle
see: trick mirror
see also: inverse proportion
I have a notebook and on it
    is a picture of a unicorn
see: fanciful
see: formidable
see: the force of wind on pines

I believe in making use
of every small thing
    a button, a nickel,
    a tomato seed,
    the sound of a creek

see: periwinkle
see: mesmerized
I watch the woodpecker work
    pecking, pointing, piercing
the call of a bird is a trill
and a sorrow

the pine stands strict against the sky
pinecones hang in bundles
see: consequential
see also: controversial
see: inner arm, under breast
    between thighs
body awareness is part
disposition, part disintegration
    part making use
of every small thing

I have a notebook and on it
    I see myself framed in letters
see: realism
see also: reality

a mirror reflects an image
deflects light
see: the color of minerals
    obsidian black
    quartz white

The Dancer Confronts the Portrait Painter

after the painting, "Madame Gaujelin," by Edgar Degas, 1867

He painted me somber—half-moon eyes clouded
by rain. He drew folded hands, fingers intertwined
like tangled roots at the edge of a dark pond.

Does he think I'm waiting for a verdict, that I'm
a branded gypsy set loose upon his couch? I am
a dancer, or used to be, my form expressed

in lithe lines, the curve of my thigh, the sigh
of shoulder. What is read in my body
but a roadmap to rapture? I am apricot

and emerald, periwinkle, fuchsia, and yet he
painted me black rendered with charcoal dust.
What eyes does he wear to draw the ebony weave

against my throat? What ears to hear my voice,
the unspoken terrors. Is that why he closed my mouth,
traced my lips a thin pink line? I should have raged

at his daring, refused to pose. I should have clawed
scarlet into obsidian, gold into umber, but instead
I held my breath, my oval face staring back at me

like a wraith. How could he see underneath
my flawless skin? How could he find me inside
this careful, choreographed dance?

Unpacking the Body Miracle

I take my uterus with me wherever I go
    miracle baby carriage
    sky-born basket of miracle fruit
downtown to the theatre
or to the bike shop in the strip mall

my uterus knows when I'm lonely
when I'm searching for a word
that means *usurper of secrets*
    miracle suitcase of cord and cordless
    small muscle miracle of rock and earth

I ask my uterus
    what is the nature of being female
and she answers with the messy particulars
of blood
    a red braid miracle of fist-sized grapefruit
    the deep well of witch and conjuring
    hysteria and hiss

I ask my doctor
    why this loss is necessary
knowing he can't guess what I've held
in the deep pocket of my belly
    a hidden power that won't be silent
    a moon-rise miracle
    miracle of timing and caves
    map of lifeline and bloodline and line
at the supermarket and the ticket counter
and the doctor's office
all the packed bodies settled
like art under glass

a few small moments to question
the ridiculous notion of saying goodbye
to a miracle
      a creation pottery
      a coral shell
the last hope I had of perfection
the last perfect home I will ever be

To the Human Barbie, From Barbie

I saw you on the internet, your waist
a narrow funnel from your chest, your hips
flared just to fit the width of bones required
to walk, to sit. Let's talk about your face—
your lineless forehead and your pouty lips,
your eyes so wide the sun could burn away
your corneas before you even blinked.
The plastic gods have done their worst to me.
I have no power, no potency, no rights.
I am a pawn, and Girlfriend, you can see
I'm not alive. My carved and plastic hands
can't hold a spoon. My rosebud mouth can't taste
sorbet. My knees won't bend, and if you must know
it's been so long since I've made love to Ken.

And then there's you, you little fool. You bought
the scam, you believed you weren't enough
the way you were. Your perfect imperfections
made you *you*—your average breasts, your cellulite,
your slightly drooping eyelids, your chipped tooth.
You weren't meant to sit upon the shelf
like me and wait for some poor girl to gaze
at ball gowns and bikinis, bleach blond hair,
and start to wonder what was wrong with her.
It's crushing, let me tell you, to watch her eyes
light up like sequins, to see her tiptoe-walk
along the aisles with tainted views of womanhood
and grace. Dear God! To take it back! To take
you back, and her, and while we're at it, me.

Therapy

The therapist wants me to unwind myself
like thread from a spool, lie flat

in grass beneath a willow. He speaks
with his measured and restrained therapist voice,

asks if I need tissues. Crying is a release,
a washing clean, a settling of heat. I listen,

because I'm supposed to listen. That's what
I'm paying him for. I want to remind him

of the private nature of pain, how it's thicker
than thread, more like 8-gauge wire, how it

refuses to be straightened. I sit in meditation,
see the hues of my breath moving between

my lungs. I feel my heartbeat in my eyes.
I know I am alive, reflected in early spring

forsythia and tulips. I cup my hands and drink
the water of my worry, my fearful wounds.

The therapist asks if I can carry stress
in my body forever, if I deserve happiness.

I watch the blue sky filter between clouds,
busy wasps building a nest in the window.

The therapist asks if I can do one good thing
for myself every day. I smile. He doesn't know

what it cost to get here. He fishes for clues—
the way I hold my hands, how my shoulders

droop, if I cross my legs when he mentions
a name. I'm listening to traffic in the street,

the urgent horns. I think about the road,
the painted yellow lines, the stones

I carry in my fist in case what unwinds
needs a weight to hold it cleanly down.

Far Away Places

There are mountains rising
above crinkled lakes, and the rivers
that fill them are glacier-fed and fast.
Crouch in the basin of river rocks, dip
your fingers in the icy cold, and feel the zip
of something bold behind your eyes—your
heart aflutter and bewildered, your breath
eager like the raging Pacific rising to full tide.

Of all the things you see here—the Kodiak,
the spawning salmon, moose with wide antlers,
herds of caribou roaming the oil pipeline—
let it be the creased coastal mountains and folded
spruce that settle you silent and awed beneath
the rain shadows. Peasant that you are, preacher,
pioneer of your own good reckoning, search
beyond permafrost to find a slip of temperate forest,
the spectral birch and deep-grained cottonwoods.

Trek across a glacier, the blue beneath you bound
in crystalline ice, absorbing every other color
so all you are is blue—sky and sea and ice—
and that slip of loneliness you always carry,
the longing for something you can't name.
Perhaps, happiness. Perhaps, contentment.
Perhaps, the glad abstractions of travel agencies
and adventure brochures: *The Experience
of a Lifetime. Find the New You when You Travel.*

Sit on a plain blue sofa, surrounded by pillows,
a journal in your lap. Pan the gold of your deepest
memories, your glittering desire. Swirl the silt
and sand away until all that's left are shiny flecks
of a bright awareness, that part of yourself
that believed long before you learned to be afraid.

The treasure's always been inside you, so near
you only needed to open your hand and let it live
upon your outstretched and eager palm.
Once you understand that, it's yours forever.

IV BROKEN: BODY

Don't argue about fairness. You'll never win that debate.

Monsieur Degas is Going Blind

He looked at us too long and now
his eyes are empty of color.
Only by rote do his hands
draw teal tulle and taffeta, magenta
overlay. He smears pastels
with his thumb, blots our features.
It was never the individuals
but the whole he loved, the whir,
the graceful allegro, the mirrored
pas de deux. He sketches a slender
torso funneled into skirt, the way
his life narrows now—light into
half-light, soon into darkness.
We watch him watching, knowing
what he sees is no longer us
but a distant blur upon the bell
of our dresses, a smear of cerulean
reflecting the stage. Once, we gathered
around him, curious to see how
he drew us, pointe and position,
battement, arabesque, but now
we avoid his paper, his dull, sad gaze.
He breaks the flow, the figure, colors
our faces too much like his own—
wide, shadowed, vacant—
nightfall too deep to dance through.

From the Balcony

I leave you sleeping and sneak outside.
From the eighth-floor hotel balcony
overlooking the Thames, I watch
tourists board cruise boats.
The river, muddy brown from its silty bottom,
swirls and churns, but the big boats handle
the sway, smooth a base for families
climbing the stairs to the exposed top deck.
It's cold and they huddle together.
Mothers hold toddlers back from the railing.
Teenagers retreat into their cell phones.
Earlier today, their captain practiced docking—
first one shore, then cross river to the other,
back and forth twelve times, each time
a new angle, each angle a new skill.
I judged him a credible sailor, his careful
delivery not once scarring boat or pier.
What the captain doesn't know is that
below the pier on the silt-edged bank,
a man pans for—surely not gold—and yet
he's down in a squat swirling
with a miner's know-how, examining
weighted particles for a glimmer, a shimmer,
something to value. What that man doesn't know
is the garbage barge on the river
that tugs a garbage trap is anchored
across from the city government building
and when the mayor looks out, he has to
look beyond the trash to see his bright city
busy with tourists. And what the mayor

doesn't know is we're all spying on each other,
comparing our fears and the dangers
of being this close to the mooring—how risky it is
to walk the thin dock, trust the boat, get in.

Flight

Juliane Koepcke, 17, was sucked out of an airplane after it was struck by lightning. She fell 2 miles to the ground still strapped to her chair and lived. She was the sole survivor of 93 passengers and crew in the crash of LANSA Flight 508 on December 24, 1971.

Can you catch me?
I'm holding the spinning insides
of a hot white light, a vortex
in brief windows, and then only steel
and wind. My breath strips sheer
as an angel's wing. I am an eagle
with a thousand talons aching
for flesh, a hawk scanning the seams
of a broken earth. I am the sudden bullet
that drops the pheasant. I give a command
and the hound howls at the scent of blood.
I am a flamingo, a blue heron, fish in the sky—
memories from the reflection of grief.
I am a red-winged blackbird, a sparrow,
a mockingbird repeating the mirrored sounds
of the living. I live.
I curve through trees, and in that final brush
of the dark, there's a holding, a stillness.

In the dark, there's a holding, a stillness
as I curve through trees, my final brush
with the living. I live
like a mockingbird repeating mirrored sounds.
I am a red-winged blackbird, a sparrow
memorizing the reflection of grief.
I am a flamingo, a blue heron, a fish in the sky.
A hound howls at the scent of blood
and I drop like a pheasant. I give a command
to the broken earth. I am a sudden bullet

in flesh, a hawk scanning seams
with a thousand talons, aching
for angel's wings. I am an eagle
in the wind. My breath strips sheer
the brief windows and then only steel
and a white light, a vortex
holding me to its spun insides.
Can you catch me?

Laundry

I washed your clothes
that smelled of urine and vomit,
twice through the cycle,
with colorfast bleach and the hottest water.

I folded them, matching
corners, sleeves. I sewed new
buttons and re-stitched hems.

I stacked them, sweatpants
and jeans, sweaters and shirts,
socks and underwear, laying
them gently, like gifts, in
a laundry basket
in your front hall

while you were
in the doctor's office,
a line of chemicals linked
to your arm.

I didn't wait for you to come home
ashen and thin, your head
wrapped in a blue bandana,
your eyes and lips

too large for words.

Mirage

    I've tried to reconcile this—
moonglow bathing the swath of countryside
near your house and you, inside, softly dying.

Was it the moon that took your flesh and hair,
buffed itself into blooming?

    Forgive me, leaving your side,
turning away from death's sounds. How they pierce—
those little shudders, that rattle, that pause.

The moon waxes fair, spreads gold
like marmalade on the toasted field.

    You call for water. I hear you
through the screen door. Death disguises its power—
faint glistening on green leaves

and the orange gladiolas, holding sweetest nectar
underneath impossible stars.

In Sickness

Two weeks, too weak to lift his head,
she spoons thin potato soup, the color of dust,
wipes the corner of his mouth, leans
to hear the slow breath in, out.

It was this the doctor warned about,
a down deep rumble, a distant storm,
and she measures the length of his face
with the fingers of a timed love. Forever,

since the day he held her hand on a walk
so far away and so close, she remembers
the pressure of his fingers on her palm, steps
in rhythm to some found place, deep and safe,

deep away, the layers below fever, beneath
sickness to the earth-path the heart knows
without sight, without proof.
His flesh rests against his bones,

heartbeat in his temple, a song
she finds strangely beautiful, but not
lasting, she knows, not lasting. There
was a time she fought the silence

in the dark flat pigment of night, raged
between the spaces of her mind
knowing what was, and his mind not
knowing what was not. Such a time

is past now, tucked against the shadows
she holds back from him. When his eyes
open, she wants him to see reflections
of a life lived long and well. So it will be,

so be it, this ending, this beginning
of the ending she bought with her love—
how the echoes move through her—
the first of the last, how quickly it comes.

Something in Walking

You trudge across the floor
in darkness, tell me the pain
won't be still and neither will you.
Something about moving
that dislodges the grip.
Something about forcing
the body forward proves you
still have some measure of control.
Pain schemes to make you still.
It's a hypnotist, a paralyzer,
a two-ton weight strapped to your back.

You leave the light off
so I can doze. Something
in that act of kindness.
You grit your teeth to keep
from moaning. Something
in that polite manner.

Something in the way
you set your feet softly
on the threaded rug from Italy,
the way you control your breathing
so I hear only a faint exhale.
It might be the tide or the wind
along a deep ridge. I know
your eyes are open. I know
there's something in the dark
defying the pain.

It's cold outside the covers.
You need a blanket around

your shoulders. I wish I could
give you one. You keep walking.
I keep wishing. Something
in wishing that keeps us both quiet.

White Magic

the time it takes / we will take it, the doctor says / these things
take time / he paces in the small examination room like he
is showing you how to wait / three steps to the door / three
back to the sink / this is how we'll do it / next month
an electromyogram after that an MRI / the doctor juggles
words on his tongue / keeps them air-strung and arching / keeps
you awestruck and speechless / you're impressed with his skill /
communication with eyes closed / but you have tricks too / you
can metamorphose into a Luna moth / eyes large on velvet
wings / the color of wound / the color of ache / you string
a tightrope from the window to the doorknob / take off
your shoes / your thighs hum like a refrigerator / your
fingers shuffle cards / you deal the doctor a full house / we
will take the time it takes, the doctor says / in the meantime
watch this / he pulls a unicycle from his pocket / spins around
the room / a nurse draws your blood / creatine phosphokinase /
anti-nuclear antibody / you write your name on the wall
with disappearing ink / the doctor says he's seen that before /
but have you seen this? / he traces a circle in his palm / presses
out the flesh / holds his hand to the window / beckons you to look
though the white mirror of his magic as if to see your future /

you see nothing but sky

Vocabulary

We're learning new words,
stretching the meaning
of prefixes, suffixes,
speaking in tongues.
The body is a complicated
word, all its impulses,
fused electrocutions.
You sit in a black recliner
that any minute could morph
into a bear, a whale, a cave.
I ask, *how are you feeling?*

I walk to the kitchen, search
the notes on neuromuscular
diseases. Disease. Dis-ease
Science has a word for it.
Myopathy. Muscle and disorder.
Dis. Apart. Asunder. Away.
A privative, negative force.
We stumble through the syllables,
stutter our calculated fears.
You ask, *how are you feeling?*
I hold my breath, tell myself
the word will come to me
if I wait for it long enough.

Insomnia Poem

watch the rise and fall of his chest
pray a trade: obedience for a rescue
tug heavy questions from a dark well
rail against unfairness: this, a sorry reward for a good life
blaspheme
pray again: forgiveness
listen to the dark house: its voice weighted with bitter syllables
replay medical terms
decipher the meanings of prefixes and suffixes
repeat a litany of drug side effects
test how the word death feels on the tongue
notice the house stretching around us, all the vacant spaces
count: not sheep or blessings, but years, weeks, days
sigh into the numbers
slide your hand to his arm like a thief
brush his skin with your fingertips
relish the deliberate warmth

Hunger

At midnight, I drag the trashcan to the fridge
and start hauling. Slimy field greens,
mold-spotted cheddar, sour milk.
I try to remember when we stopped eating—
the day your diagnosis unraveled us or before that,
when your symptoms bulged out of the box
we made for them. How long we listened
to your body's complaint, its voice raw
and tangled like the sprouts I toss in the can.
And now the shriveled strawberries. And now
the thinly-sliced honey ham. And now
the trashcan is full and the fridge empty
except for a few items with long shelf lives:
coffee creamer, mustard, balsamic vinaigrette.
Look at the woman I've become, scrawny
with watching you suffer, starved for answers.
Who has the energy to swallow?
Your meager mouth chews and chews a cud of words:
How could this happen? How can this be?
We've nearly disappeared, our eyes too large
for our sunken bodies, our cheeks hollow, our bellies
stretched across the bones of a future we're afraid
to speak. I tie up the trash, take it outside to the curb.
A harvest moon rises like an open mouth,
wide and hungry above the empty street.

Airport Pat-Down

returning home from Mayo Clinic

I wipe my face with the sleeve of my coat
as you stand with your arms stretched out like a cross.
A security guard runs his hands down your scars,
his wide, hard hands pat-down your chest.

You stand with your arms spread out like a cross
as he pats-down your shoulder, bandaged and raw.
His strong, hard hands on your newly-split chest,
your needle-wrecked arms, your bruised fingertips.

He pats-down your shoulder, biopsied and raw.
He towers above you, expressionless, cancer-less.
With muscular arms and blue-gloved fingers,
he pats-down your fragile ribs, pats-down your belly.

He towers in front of you, merciless, cancer-less,
pats-down your hips, your crotch, your legs,
your just-opened ribs, your ravaged belly.
He turns you, examines your pale, cracked hands.

He pats-down your hips, your thighs, your calves,
proving you innocent, declaring you harmless.
He turns you, finished. I reach for your hand.
We walk down the terminal to our gate.

He proved you're innocent, that dying is harmless.
The security guard nods, his hands in his pockets.
As we walk the long terminal to our gate,
I dry my eyes on the sleeve of my coat.

Telling the Family There is Nothing More They Can Do

What used to be a mouthful
is now a murmur in distant tongues,
a soft-edged flutter in throats.
What used to be a circle is now
a gathering in the snow,
the language bone-cold.
We said they could say anything
except *I'm sorry*. We have no use
for sympathy, no need for regret.
We've enough sad smiles lining
the back of the bookshelf,
lazy curves slinking thin spirals.
We watch their faces fall
and break in the slush.
They bend to retrieve them,
pass around the remains, share
the crumbs with dogs.
It's hard to watch them try so hard,
shuffle words, deal them in a new order
but always the bank gets blackjack,
always the coin lands on tails.
Vultures spin in the thermals above them.
We rescue them from the cage of sadness,
show them the silver latch works
equally well from the inside. They fold
their bodies backwards—an origami dance
of swans gliding across silver meadows
to mellow houses. We are alone again.
We gather white shadows,
pretend to feast.

V Broken: Heart

Forgive me, but sometimes I tire of weeping.

Ars Poetica

Curve yourself backwards
until your loneliness
feels dangerous and you ache
in the marrow of your bones.

Now, wander.

The river and trees offer a clue
to your sorrows. Pull the cloak
of the earth around you
and settle in its fierce threads.
Your heart unravels
and is lovelier
for the wrecking of it.

Morning Practice

My dog follows the sun as it streams
through windows in the French door.
  Low and from the east, heat toasts
  the cushions on the wing back, simmers
the carpet in elongated squares. My dog
knows the posture for these mornings.
  Stretched out and mellow, she dreams
  the lazy life of this sedated routine.
She is aging. In dog years, she marks
fifty-six, not that far from my own
  labor of years. Sometimes I feel the weight
  of them, yearn for time to settle
in the warm light and sleep. But now,
in the center of a spreading awareness,
  between the sharp edges of children
  leaving home and parents going home,
there is no time for such luxury.
There are so many to miss.

I balance the strangeness of this raw unknown
with the succor of custom—
  hazelnut creamer in my coffee,
  a memorized Psalm, the angle of light
my dog seeks to soften the new day.
Later, we will walk the path between
  our door and the vast mystery
  of this life. She will catch the scent
of squirrels and I will ponder
how to bridge change with a measure
  of grace. We circle the mesh
  of coneflower and yarrow, tease

the koi with our shadows, search
for the brown thrasher hidden deep
    within the pine. This is the secret
    to enduring—each day,
a sip of peace. The kindness we give ourselves
might just be enough to save us.

Letter to David from Onyx Cave

I'm disappointed there's no onyx—
only striated calcite grooved with the flow
of water as it drapes the ceilings and walls.
I walk the yellow line painted on the concrete ramp
leading deep into the belly of stone, and I think
of the boy found living in a cave near here.
He had to be coaxed out like a kitten,
promised things—a bed, warm milk.

I walk between ledges stacked like shelves in a morgue.
I wonder if that boy curved his back against stone,
his ragged sleeping bag a cocoon against the voices
in his head. When he opened his eyes, was there
any difference in what he could sense? Was there
only dark and cold and damp and lonely?
Or was there a sort of kinship, a map of home.

The banded flowstone, despite its girth and age,
is delicate, a crystal bone. The oil from a single human
fingerprint is enough to divert its living water, cause
it to crumble. I think about you, David—your eggshell
heart thin and easily broken, your childhood
an excavation of loss. If I push the red button
on the metal box ahead, I can listen to an explanation—

how water carves the world, creates shapes
our imagination names: here, masks of comedy
and tragedy, there, a camel holding the earth on its back.
And you, dear David, how long until your heart
gives out from the load your carry, before your veil
of wit and excuses crumbles and your cave of language
won't hide you anymore? Can you let yourself
be discovered, come out squinting in the sun?

Can you turn your back on the echo of all that pain?

Ghosts Use Logic to Convince My Mother They Exist

My mother doesn't believe in ghosts
but the ghosts have other plans.

Whooshes of white light spin around her dark bedroom,
her newly dead brother, a dove freed from pain,
exuberant in new glory.

She is not afraid
but the light keeps her awake. She tells stories
from her childhood, how her brother was a slight child
and sickly, how she busted the noses of bullies
who laughed at his awkward gait. The light fades contented.

At a hotel in Abingdon, we sit in the lobby and listen
to talk about galloping hooves and a woman's moans.
The Civil War dead limp down hallways, remnants
of their former selves. They stand at attention along paths
outside, leaning for orders never given. They listen,
but are loud in their listening—a rustle, a shuffle, a hiss.

We ask how likely it is to see a ghost
and a woman tells us we'll never see one if we don't believe.
Somewhere between the walls, a horse neighs and snorts.

At the cemetery where her brother lies under fresh dirt,
my mother tries to explain the light as some kind of prism
snatched by the moon. In the photo, a man's figure
stands behind her, his face shrouded in cloud.

When asked to explain, my mother hesitates,
rations her answer with reservations, but the white flash
on her shoulder, in the shape of a hand,
denies any doubt, as does the warmth she remembers
and the damp feeling of loss she carries now.

Tangles

What I want to know is
why, every night, I chase
memories of my mother
through dreams. And why,
when I reach out my hand
to pick the feathery plumes
of maiden grass, they slide
through my fingers like birds.

What I want
is to take back a few years
and turn at the last crossroads
where my mother is standing
with a mind clear of tangles,
and I can show her a handful
of flowers and ask for their names
and she can whisper
bee balm, alstroemeria, aster,
and I can say, *yes, I knew that,
I should have remembered,*
and she can say, *I'm here
to not let you forget.*

Then, those dark afternoons
when the sky is hosting
a show of rain and lightning,
and the bluebells in the far
meadow are raked across
the confused, tumbled ground,
I won't feel as though
I'm still hoping to pick
the last rose before the wind strips
my mother's fading mind.

I want to know how to find it,
save it. I want to know
how to give it back.

Darker

He sits in the home office, staring
past his computer to the pin oak
framed in the window. It's not
a healthy tree, though it was
in its time, tall and wide, shading
the side yard. Now, there's more
dead than live branches and he studies
the slow randomness of dying—
the high, the low—the balance
of light. I know what he's thinking
when he sits like that, still and weighted
with the kind of grief that holds
its own hand, won't be comforted
by anything else. He is watching
his mother die a little more every day.
I've told him it's ok to rest, to sleep
one morning past the first glimmer
of sunrise. He carries private shadows
like a stack of books, opens them, runs
his fingers down stiff pages, bears each
broken spine. He is learning what it means
to suffer beneath the flesh of the body,
the heart with its constant hollow space
speared with the turning of hours.
It's almost dusk. He allows himself
this brief silence, this small reprieve
as daylight shifts under the dying oak.
He doesn't notice the minutes passing,
the room growing darker and darker.

Nightfall

how many times
death comes
as a dark mist
inching across grass
we blink, rub our eyes
the image fades

you stand
in your hospital gown
laughing, barefoot
your head tilted
your hair disarrayed

you say something
called from the window
and you were scared
but you climbed
out of bed, parted
the blinds, saw only dusk
draping a sweater
over the fading day

your face bears
a sweet innocence
eighty-one years
tucked and smoothed
your voice, a bright beacon
explaining
you're not sleepy yet

Waiting

The wind howls through the keyhole
and the creek is inches from escaping
its walls. More rain expected.

High water and mud. The trees tremble
against a ghost-gray sky. It is winter
and I sit in a faded corduroy La-Z-Boy

fingering the folds of the fabric. My mother
is dying. My sister is pacing, first to the walls
of the bedroom, then to the hall, worrying

a path in a room that smells like eucalyptus
and lavender, forever the scent of death now.
In the end, the body wins, or loses,

depending on how you look at it,
but that's the price of being wrapped
in flesh, of being wound by the rhythm

of blood. Thunder murmurs,
then rain pounds the roof, hollows
the yard into a deep darkness, a thick

suction of rock and loam. We've put
the clock away. Better to count our sorrows
than hours. It seems less than respectful

to keep a log of time so we let the dark
tell us to doze, the bleak sun to wake.
Every so often, one of us cries, a flash flood,

and we let it wash the room of its weight.
It's necessary to breathe, we tell each other,
even as we wait for that one still moment

when breath becomes plain air settling
into cupped hands, and silence a prize
we beg for her sake, dread for our own.

In my Dream

          you are dead
and now, awake, I must feel
the solid floor beneath my feet.
I shake loose the ghostly sheets,
quick-step to the kitchen.
I reach to turn on the light,
but I'm afraid of what I'll see,

the remembrance, so plain
and reckless on the counter,
the 23rd Psalm, your name, dates
that grip years,

or a shadow, yours, mine,
pinned to the cheery yellow wall,
stunned, as if anything could happen
and did.

Traveling North with Grief

Winter. My breath, a mist rising
beneath yellow tamarack trees.
The wind shifts. Golden needles
float down, spear my hair.
I am decorated with death.
I walk by the lake. Ice-crusted sand.
Footprints of a dog. Brown speckled
stones. I am thirty miles from Canada,
a thousand miles from your body
in warmer ground. I name the face
I see in the mirror, Winter. I open
my coat, let what's bitter and clean
burn through me. A winter reckoning.
The winter, brittle, star-torn wreck of me.
Someone lit a fire in a cabin. Wood smoke
filters with memory of flame. And the lake
shifts in its shallow banks. And the tamaracks
glitter. The narrow trail is braided
with roots. The promise of an overlook.
I practiced grief for a decade. Now,
from the heights, against the jagged edge
of mountain, I call for you. The white sky
swallows your name. A single offering.
I thought the cold would mock me.
I wanted the cold to ruin me. I owed you
that much. To suffer in remembrance.
A winter banishment. The papery skin
of river birch. The aspen trembling.
The wordless yellow-gold tamaracks
listening. And winter kissing the sky-stung
silence as if love could solve everything.

Poison Ivy

Once you see it, it's too late,
your mother always said.
The vine climbed on and through
the stone wall, shiny, the kind
of green that made you think
vibrant and healthy, and though
you didn't think you touched it,
when the first red bump appeared,
you knew you must have.
You wanted to call your mom and say
      I've got a problem
and describe it because that's
what you'd always done
when something bad happened.
She'd listen, say
      poison ivy,
then say you need steroids
because she remembers the last time
you laid on the couch with blisters
trailing up your legs, something
you'd forgotten because you knew
she'd remind you. That's what
mothers do. Tell you what's wrong
and how to fix it. Remind you.

And then you remembered,
just as you were about to pick up
the phone, that your mother is gone,
dead three months, and you'll chastise
yourself for thinking *dead* again,
because it's better to say *passed away,*
though you're pretty sure your mother
wouldn't care which one you said.

In your mind you said
         passed, passed, passed
as if you needed to remember, then
something wild and poisonous
climbed inside you and you sat
with your calamine and ice pack
and cried just like you did that day
everything became clear.

Your mother wasn't coming home
and you didn't say the things you
wanted to say because your heart,
your muted heart, caved in upon itself
as you watched your mother pass
through the process of death.
         There's a process,
the hospice nurses told you
and here's what we see in your mother
and then you saw it too, as if a lens
focused on the right places made
everything obvious. You imagined
your mother shaking her head as she
examined your arm.
         It's obvious. See the red streak
         where the leaf brushed skin?

You'd tell her you didn't see
this coming. She'd say you don't know
what you don't know until you know it,
and smile that luminous smile of hers
that made you think every bad thing
was fixable, until the one that wasn't,
and it was yours to handle, yours alone.

What I Carry

This is not rare & I am not
a spectacle carrying grief this way,
over my shoulder, though it spills
thick & red down my back.

My hair is tangled like a nest
but useless for birds & on my arms
are punctures from fingernails,
little moons arcing.

I appear a silhouette in mist
on the busy beach, stumbling
through deep sand. I walk
cold waves to my thighs.

Mothers with tow-headed toddlers,
the chubby teenager with a frisbee,
the old man with a chest of white hair
stop & nod at what I carry—

      a body
of loss folding its wings,
tucking its trembling face
against my neck.

All of this is commonplace
& unsurprising, being human,
so I sit in the cold sand
to collect my strength

& wait until my heart slows
enough to catch my breath.
I stand then, test the wind,
walk on with my load.

Advice after Losing a Spouse

For M.

For now, breathe.
No need to get ambitious.
Let morning roll over you,
taste the salt, the grit. Find shade.
Maybe that slim birch just learning
to sway, kneading the silt of creek bed.
Maybe the white oak with acorn caps
still attached to top branches.
You might find squirrels. Squirrels are good.
Don't try to take in the sky—it's too wide and high.
You have to sip first, then swallow,
stepwise, methodical. It's best to go slow.
When you find the cliff, the crumbling
limestone shelves, when your toes hang over
the edge of the high dive,
I've found crows can be helpful—
the sleek wings, glossy eyes seeking
the hidden glitter, scouring the high grass
for silver keys, blue glass, a bronze coin.
Distraction works for a time—give yourself
those freebies. The cost is high for the rest.
You'll want to save, budget for the days
that take risk, the boulder and avalanche,
all that snow and ice.
You'll daydream a lot, shuffle wishes
with might-have-been's.
That's natural. Don't fight it.
But don't argue about fairness.
You'll never win that debate.
Find yourself a cherry tree instead,
stand within its sheltered canopy, behind

its fringed and fragrant curtain where the light
is dim and the air is clean and kind.
Breathe and breathe.
Stay as long as you need to.

Re-Wilding

The forest is reclaiming the back pasture.
Trees inch step by ancient step across
the clotted grass. Years ago, cows clipped
sturdy blades to the root. Mud streamed,
ankle deep, when it rained. I stand
at field edge and think of containment,
ponder why a fence line with a corner gate
seems vital. The wind spreads wildflowers
with a random breath. I counted breaths
before my mother died. I counted the seconds
between each rattled pull. In the final silence,
when there was nothing left of my mother to count,
I counted the beats of my own quick heart.

A heart of wilderness tames the desire
for order. Every morning, deer risk the road
to graze in the sheltered field. I measure
in brown-earth eyes a certain understanding
of danger, of death. A deer dies with its eyes open.
What afterworld is it searching for, what reward?
What random thought but an instinct to run?

I run the fence line, stomping the tangled weeds.
My socks are decorated with prickly burrs.
I am a vehicle to a foreign place where the sun
bleaches the past. The forest is hungry, eager
to swallow the open spaces. I'm hungry
for something I can't reach, can't name.
In a hidden glade, white wildflowers carpet
the thin soil between limestone flats.
I remember my mother's face pulled back
against its bones. Seedlings at the end
of the pasture breathe the sun. Wildflowers fan
in the wind—bright, star-shaped, uncountable.

To Make Sense of this World Again

I want to see something small—a pumpkin seed
in the beak of a crow, an accidental release
and a turning of soil. A sprout, pale green. A leaf,
an anchoring tendril. A floppy yellow flower and bees.

I'm willing to stand in pine straw and listen to bullfrogs
groan as they crouch by a pond encumbered with string
algae. There's so little space allowed for the untamed.
A rogue pumpkin vine stretches to the fence, curves

under oak leaf hydrangeas, reappears with an orb
of green swollen with carotenoids firing in the sun.
The garden becomes an altar to orange, the tangled
vine, a labyrinth of questions: How? When? Why?

Sometimes I'm shadowed by the state of this world,
its dark edges, its darker heart. What good I try to do
is casually undone by jaded voices speaking careless words.
Forgive me, but sometimes I tire of weeping.

Oh, let me have my fleshy rind, my fearless, porous stalk.
Let me follow the breath of dragonflies, the toeprints
of salamanders, the box turtle's gameboard shell. There's
little enough reward for wishes and love's too often washed

with spit. I struggle with the weight of the largest pumpkin,
marvel at its beautiful heft. There are six now, squatting
like wayward gifts. It takes something simple, unexpected,
something that proves its place by arriving uninvited,

by daring to be seen between the dogwood and coneflowers.
I want to see a harvest rising from the rubbish. I want
to hold it in my hands as proof there are small things
that have no business growing, but they grow anyway.

Notes

"The Clock Master" is a villanelle and was written as a piece of fantasy about the cleaning of the Breslin Tower Clock at The University of the South, Sewanee, TN. Of course, the poem is also a message about time itself and who controls the length of our lives on earth.

"After Midnight," "The Pact," and "Into Morning" were written in response to a news article about a suicide pact between two teenage girls.

"Deputy Finch" was written in response to an incident which occurred on the Natchez Trace Bridge (dubbed "The Suicide Bridge") in Williamson County, TN.

"Running" was written in response to a school shooting in Parkland, Florida, in which 17 people died.

"Begonia" was written in response to a 2017 shooting incident at a small country church in Smyrna, TN, which killed one person.

"Seven Ways of Looking at a Shooting" was inspired by the art piece "Anxious Audience," 2016 by Rashid Johnson. This painting was part of the "Chaos and Awe" Exhibit at the Frist Art Museum in Nashville, TN.

"Miss Landmine" was written in response to a magazine article about a beauty pageant for landmine victims in Angola.

"How to Spell America" was written in response to my experience as a volunteer tutor with Nashville Adult Literacy Council, in which I worked with immigrants to improve their English language skills.

"If You Know What's Good for You" was written in response to a conversation with a friend. I recalled a memory of listening to suspected domestic abuse in an apartment complex thirty years ago. My friend shared experiences of witnessing her mother's abuse by a boyfriend. The sad thing is many of us could tell similar stories.

"Marbles" was written in response to a photograph of my daughter when she was about 6 years old. A mibster is a person who plays the game of marbles and/or collects marbles. This poem contains many unusual words relating to playing the game as well as naming the various kinds of marbles. My daughter did not play the game in the usual sense. She created masterful works of art using marbles as her medium.

"Photograph" was written as an Ekphrastic exercise from an old photo found in an antique shop.

"Poem in Which My Body is a Ransom" relays a confusing 3-month experience when I was 18 years old and worked a server in an upscale restaurant. I still have Anthony's card somewhere.

"Hope" is an Ekphrastic poem written in response to the painting by Gustav Klimt titled "Hope II." This painting is in the collection of the Museum of Modern Art in New York City. A description of the painting from the MoMA website says: "A pregnant woman bows her head and closes her eyes, as if praying for the safety of her child. Peeping out from behind her stomach is a death's head, a looming sign of the danger she faces. At her feet, three women with lowered heads raise their hands, presumably also in prayer—although their solemnity might also imply mourning, as if they foresaw the child's fate."

"Eve Decides Motherhood Is Not All It's Cracked Up to Be" and "Eve Contemplates a Name Change" are from a series of poems I wrote depicting the biblical Eve as a contemporary woman facing the challenges of marriage and motherhood.

"The Dancer Confronts the Portrait Painter" is an Ekphrastic poem written in response to the painting "Madame Gaujalin" by Edgar Degas in 1867. The painting hangs in the Isabella Stewart Gardner Museum in Boston. Commentary regarding the painting says: "Joséphine Gaujelin (or Gozelin) was a dancer at the Opéra in Paris and later an actor at the Théâtre du Gymnase. In this portrait, she appears in street clothes, sitting in her dressing room.

Wrapped entirely in black, she sits rigidly, with arms clenched to her sides. The dour expression and reserved demeanor belie her reputation as a charismatic beauty. The portrait is almost deliberately unglamorous, although the intensity of the sitter's gaze is compelling, if not disconcerting to some viewers. Gaujelin, who had commissioned the portrait, rejected it."

"Flight" is written as a type of mirror poem in which the lines of the second stanza are reflected in reverse order from the first stanza. Liberties are taken within the line so the wording is not exact which results in variations of meaning between the two stanzas.

"Airport Pat-Down" was written in response to a personal experience at Rochester International Airport in Rochester, MN.

"Traveling North with Grief" was written in northern Idaho, where the tamarack trees grow tall. Tamaracks, also known as larch trees, are deciduous conifers that turn golden yellow and lose their needles in autumn. They are among the dominant plants in the boreal forests.

Acknowledgements

The author would like to express deep appreciate to the editors of the following journals within which these poems first appeared, sometimes in slightly different forms.

Barren Magazine – "Poem in Which My Body is a Ransom"

Boxcar Poetry Review – "Begonia"

CEO Literary Magazine – "Photograph"

Chiron Review – "Flight," "Seven Ways of Looking at a Shooting," and "Peacock Hill"

Door is a Jar – "Therapy" and "Nightfall"

Dragon Poet Review – "Hematology"

Eunoia Review – "It's My Birthday and I'm Thinking About Death"

Euphemism – "Discovering Sex"

Feminine Collective – "To the Human Barbie, From Barbie"

Freedom Papers – "If Freedom"

Ghost City Review – "Advice after Losing a Spouse"

The Inflectionist Review – "Running"

Jelly Bucket – "Monsieur Degas is Going Blind"

Linden Avenue Literary Journal – "To Make Sense of This World Again"

Main Street Rag – "Definition of Middle Age," "From the Balcony," and "Hunger"

Negative Capability Press – "Letter to David from Onyx Cave"

Number One – "Playing Dead," "Morning Practice" "Miss Landmine" and "In Sickness"

PanoplyZine – "What Words Cost"

Remington Review – "Darker"

River and South Review – "Laundry"

Sky Island Journal – "How to Spell America," (nominated for a Pushcart Prize and Best of the Net), "Tangles," and "Shopping for Sweaters"

Sow's Ear Poetry Review – "Marbles"

Spank the Carp – "The Pact"

Stirring, A Literary Collection – "Traveling North with Grief"

Subprimal Poetry Art – "Into Morning"

Synaeresis Arts and Poetry – "A Dream" and "Facts About Lightning" (nominated for a Pushcart Prize.)

Treehouse: An Exhibition of the Arts – "Ghosts use Logic to Convince My Mother They Exist"

Special Thanks

To the poets with whom I share friendship and those who I do not know personally, yet live in kinship and solidarity because of the power of their words: Thank you for calling the world to attention, for being brave enough to reveal both brokenness and wholeness, and for clearing the path between them with poems.

To Ruth Thompson and Don Mitchell of Saddle Road Press: What a sweet ride to work on this book with you! Thank you for believing in me.

To my fellow editors and the contributing poets of Rockvale Review and the writers of Rockvale Writers' Colony: You are my blessing and my joy.

To the poets of Black Dog Poetry Open Mic, Rockvale Poetry Book Club, and Daydream Believers Critique Group: You sustain me, you teach me, you challenge me. I am grateful.

To the creative geniuses of West of the Moon Creative Retreat: Way back in 2012, something "clicked" for me. All I have done and become since then is in part due to what I learned from you—to believe in my creativity, to affirm my writing dreams, to be confident in who I am and what I do. My experiences at WOTM were a precious gift. Thank you.

To Bill and Suzanne Brown: You are my mentors in poetry and life, my heart, and my poetry home. You mean more to me than you will ever know.

And to you, Readers: The places in you and in your life that make you feel broken, confused, grief-stricken, anguished, can be the same places that will lead to change, growth, belief, and renewed strength. You have to face them, name them, and bring them into the light. May these poems inspire in you a rising-up and a sending-forth. May they be part of the flagstones that pave the road back to yourself. Keep going, dear ones.

About the Author

Sandy Coomer is a poet, artist, Ironman athlete, and social entrepreneur from Nashville, TN. Her poetry has been published in numerous journals and she is the author of three poetry chapbooks and a full-length collection, *Available Light* (Iris Press). She is a multiple Pushcart Prize and Best of the Net nominee and her poem, "Calligraphy" was a 2019 Best of the Net finalist.

Ashley Sarmiento

Sandy is a past poetry mentor in the AWP Writer to Writer Mentorship Program and the founding editor of the online poetry journal Rockvale Review.

She is the founder and director of Rockvale Writers' Colony in College Grove, TN, a not-for-profit organization that exists to support and educate writers of all genres and backgrounds.

She is a teacher, a dreamer, and an explorer. Her favorite word is "believe."

www.ingramcontent.com/pod-product-compliance
Lightning Source LLC
Chambersburg PA
CBHW020910080526
44589CB00011B/534